Business 110B - SJSU
Rich Burkhard
Spring 2010

Bollywood Box Office: Planning for Systems that Make the World's Largest Film Industry Work

Background

Exotic Filmcraft Bombay Productions (EFBP) is a service group that designs, develops and delivers interior and exterior set materials for the television, film, and theatre industries in the greater Mumbai area in India. Their customers include such well known TV programs and many film producers that are based in the West Bombay Valley. In their designs, they use a mixture of commonly available props, furniture, plastic plants, and imported rare and exotic props, cars, and other materials. *EFBP* is a women-owned business that employs thirty-two people and has gross revenues of 1,564,559,967 Rupees ($36 million) with a before-tax profit of $5.2 million. Richa Shrivastava and Mia Avocado own the majority of the business, along with several investors who have taken a minority interest. Richa, a set designer, manages the artistic side of the business, including not only supervising the design activity, but also job production and the selection of vendors. Mia is the general manager who manages the inventory and supervises the sales and financial activities.

Design Procedures

EFBP's Design Group employs six full-time set designers; an administrative assistant, Edward Kim; a prop specialist, and a group manager, Crystal Nguyen. Crystal works closely with Richa, who remains the firm's chief set designer. This arrangement could be problematic except that Crystal and Richa have worked together for many years, and they have established a relationship in which Crystal manages the more administrative concerns of the design group while Richa oversees and contributes to the major design activities.

Each set designer potentially has many projects that s/he works on, and each project potentially has many set designers. After one of *EFBP's* salespeople has identified a real prospect, the set designers meet with clients to determine the client's requirements. Depending on the size and complexity of a project, the set designers may produce one or more preliminary sketches. They also prepare a formal Design Bid that contains a general description of the project, a list of props and materials, and a detailed list of both material and labor prices, including the price for any set designer hours required after the bid has been approved.

EFBP contacts a client for pre-bid-approval design time only if the project is exceptionally large or risky; in all other cases, the costs of preparing the Design Bid are factored into *EFBP's* markup for props, materials, *and* production-phase labor. Gary, the Design Group manager, must approve the Design Bid before it is shown to the client.

After the client has approved the bid, the set designers develop formal sketches and blueprints, and Richa forms a team to implement the project. This team usually consists of the salesperson who initiated contact with the client, one or more set designers, and several members from Production. In a large project, the Design and Production Group managers, as well as Richa herself, are members of the team. Because teams cut across the horizontal organization, there are no rigid, formal lines of authority. For example, the project team assigned to the "Jackie Chan – On Ice" project includes a sales representative, Timon Brown; a set designer, Taimur Singh; the Production Group manager, Linda Yen; and the production workers, Shawn Mig and Vladimir Popeyeski.

After the design has been approved and the final sketches and blueprints drawn, the set designer's role is primarily that of a project overseer. For more complicated projects, the set designer regularly inspects the progress of the Production crew to ensure that the design is being implemented on schedule and to specifications. The set designer may also need to meet with the client if changes to the approved bid are requested.

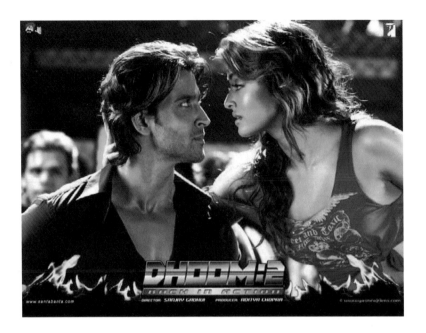

Production Process

The Production Group implements the set designs. This group consists of the manager, Linda Yen; three set-builders; three laborers; and two drivers. The personnel in this group are assisted by outside specialists (for example, heavy equipment operators) and by part-time contract laborers. Production's work requires trucks, equipment, tools, supplies, materials, and props. The vehicles, equipment, and tools must be moved from site to site.

With many projects under way simultaneously, the scheduling of workers, equipment, and tools is critical. Linda is responsible for using the set designer's bid and blueprint to generate a Production Plan. Data provided in the Production Plan includes information on the scheduling of labor and material delivery, project task completion dates, and other implementation data. Linda submits each Production Plan to Richa for approval before the plan is implemented. Richa returns the approved Production Plan to Linda, who makes a copy and submits it to Edward for filing and tracking. If a client requests changes to the design after production has begun, the set designer prepares a revised bid and submits it to Linda. Linda augments the revised bid with production data to generate a revised Production Plan and sends the revised plan to Richa for approval.

Project Costs

Except for very small jobs, each set designer (or the lead set designer in the case of a larger project requiring two or more set designers) is required to submit a budget,of the time she expects to devote to preparing the bid (see sample Design Budget). The Design Budget is submitted to Richa for approval after a preliminary meeting with a client so that the set designer can realistically estimate the hours required to design each project.

EFBP has a general policy that its set designers may invest approximately 10 percent of the potential project's bid amount in design activities; thus, for a project with an estimated bid of $15,500, the maximum design hours is 19 ($100 per set designer hour * 19 = $1900, or approximately 15 percent of the bid amount). Richa and Mia instituted this policy because set designers tended to get carried away and to invest more design time in a bid than management deemed appropriate.

EFBP uses two forms to track the actual costs of materials and labor for each project. Production workers submit a Set Preparation Statement of Work (SPSW), indicating the material and labor expended on each project each day. Notice that as a control measure, Nastia Liukin, the Prop warehouse clerk, must indicate the cost of all props and materials and must approve their removal from inventory. In addition, each set designer submits a Daily Work Report (DWR) indicating the hours devoted to each of his or her projects.

Copies of all forms -- Design Bid, Production Plan, Design Budget, Production Daily Work Report, and Set designer Daily Work Report - are submitted to Kim Edward, the Design Group administrative assistant, on a daily basis. At the start of every business day, Kim records the bid amount from new or revised Design Bids, the estimated production costs for labor and materials from new or revised Production Plans, and the actual costs of material and labor for each project from Production Daily Work Reports and Set designer Daily Work Reports. Each Monday morning, Kim summarizes this data in a report showing the estimated and actual costs to date for each project and delivers it to Mia, Richa, the Group managers, and the set designers.

Notice that the Production Plan, Production Daily Work Report, Set designer Daily Work Report, and Project Administration Report track *EFBP's* actual direct costs for a project. For example, the actual cost per hour of a laborer or set designer and the net cost of materials and props are used to compute and track how much *EFBP* has actually spent on a project. In general, *EFBP* expects that direct costs will consume between 50 and 70 percent of the amount bid for each project.

EFBP needs to track actual costs because, once the bid has been approved, *EFBP* is committed to complete the project for the amount bid. Thus, if the net cost of props and materials increases or the set designers or laborers invest more time than expected, *EFBP* must absorb the added costs. Clients are responsible for extra charges only if they change the design after the bid has been approved.

Project Administration System

Currently, *EFBP* has made only limited use of information technology to improve its efficiency and effectiveness. The set designers have access to one microcomputer and a laser printer, which they use to prepare design bids. Kim, who is taking evening classes at the local university to complete an Business degree with a concentration in MIS, recently developed an Excel spreadsheet template to help the set designers prepare design bids and to improve the format consistency and the mathematical accuracy of this form. Kim also has a microcomputer; she uses an Excel spreadsheet to maintain data about bid amounts and estimated and actual costs of each project; she uses Microsoft Word for Windows to generate reports. Kim would like to develop an Excel spreadsheet to generate the Project Administration report, but hasn't found the time. She shares the Design Group laser printer. A third microcomputer, a second laser printer, and another Excel template are used by Linda Yen, the Production Group manager, to produce a Production Plan.

Starting the Project

One particularly stressful week, Kim worked overtime three evenings and a Saturday morning to enter all the project data. As she delivered her weekly Project Administration Report to Mia Monday morning, Kim commented on her increasing workload. "Do you have a minute, Mia?" "Sure, Kim. Have a seat," Mia offered, clearing a stack of papers from a chair for Kim. "What can I do for you?"

"Mia, I'm going crazy. I know it's not your problem that I've chosen to take classes a couple nights a week to complete my degree. But I'm finding it increasingly difficult to give my classes the attention they require because I so often have to work overtime to complete all my duties here at *EFBP*."

"I've noticed you've been staying late pretty often. In fact, weren't you here late last Tuesday? I thought you had a class Tuesday nights."

"I do, but I felt I had to miss the first hour so that I'd have those reports you asked for ready by noon the next day."

"Sorry about that. You need to learn to say 'No' or to tell me to take a hike, Kim. You're an excellent worker, but I don't want you to jeopardize your degree on our account. But, I hope you'll understand my pleasure in telling you that I don't expect things to change. This has been a banner year for *EFBP*, and I expect our sales to continue their upward trend. Unfortunately, that means more bids, plans, reports, etc. for you. Do you *think* we should hire another assistant for the Design Group?"

"I'm not sure, at this point, that the workload justifies another body. Perhaps *a* part-timer." Seeing Mia grimace, Kim added, "I know we've had bad luck with part-time staff; but something has to give."

"I understand your situation, Kim, but, as you *said,* we don't seem to get the commitment from part-timers that *EFBP* requires. And, by the time we pay benefits, profit-sharing, and a decent salary to attract a reliable part-time worker, we end up spending almost as much as we would for a full-time employee."

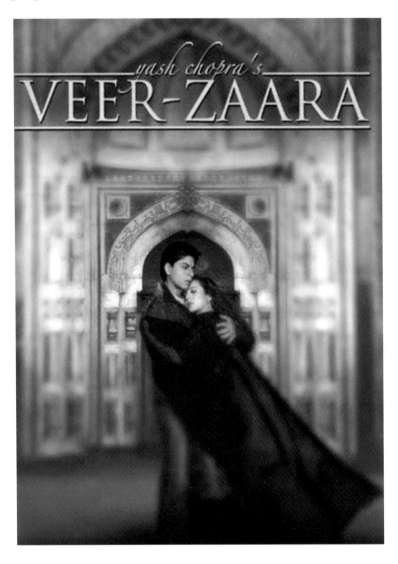

"Not to be nosy, but what would a part-time worker cost *EFBP* each year?"

"Well, Kim, I hardly think I'd be betraying a trade secret by telling *you* that, with insurance, worker's comp, unemployment, social security, etc., you cost about $85,000 a year. A part timer would be closer to $35 - 40,000."

"Then maybe there's a good alternative to hiring another employee. You know, I'm studying management information systems. I'm no expert -- not yet, anyway -- but I bet it would cost you less in the long term to solve this problem by improving our information systems. We could automate the most time-consuming and repetitive part of my job, all the tedious *data entry*. Or redistribute it so that instead of set designers and production workers filling out paper forms, they'd enter the data about costs and hours on a data entry screen. That way, I wouldn't have to reenter all their data. Not only would that save time but it would also reduce errors."

"True, but it would probably cost a small fortune to implement such a system."

"Not necessarily. We already have some of the hardware required. And the *system isn't* so large or complex that we'd need a heavy-duty consultant. In fact, we could get a lot of the work done at no cost."

"Kim, you must be crazy! Haven't you heard the expression, *There's no free lunch, even if you're a homeless person outside of McDonald's?*"

"Maybe, maybe not. My systems development prof is looking for projects for student groups to complete. It might take longer than if we hired a consultant, and a student group might not be able to do all the work. But we could determine the requirements, do the initial design, and implement a prototype or at least the simpler pieces of a production system. And the prof supervises all the students' work, so you wouldn't have to worry about wasting a lot of time and ending up with a bum system. What do you say?"

"I say I need to talk with your instructor and with other businesses that have sponsored student projects, then we'll see."

After consulting with Richa and contacting several local businesses that had been involved in student projects, Mia decided to approve Kim's idea. However, in talking with Kim's instructor, Mia set several conditions for *EFBP's* involvement: (1) Kim must serve as the project leader and keep *EFBP* administration informed of the team's progress; (2) the students must confine their investigation to *EFBP's* cost tracking processes; (3) any system proposal must incorporate *EFBP's* existing hardware, must not exceed $100,000 for the purchase of hardware and software and for the construction and installation of the complete system; and (4) it should be feasible to implement the proposed system within 2-3 months after the initial analysis and design have been completed.

Interviews with EFBP Users

Interview with Satya Swami, Set designer

The student project group, lead by Kim Edward, met with Satya to determine how the set designers would interact with the Project Administration System. Kim began by asking Satya how he prepares a Design Bid (see Design Bid).

Design Bid

"For your purposes, I guess the most relevant information concerns how I determine the bid amount. Estimating the total price of props and materials is pretty clear cut. Kim distributes an updated price list for all inventory items with each day's inventory report. All I do is find the desired item on the price list.

Once I have found the first item in the price list I open the spreadsheet template that Kim created. After the spreadsheet is opened I rename the spreadsheet with the project name and version number. For example, if you look at the Design Bid example, I would name the spreadsheet LS Mall V01. I fill in all of the client information, their name, address, city, state and zip. I also fill in the client contact and their phone number. Next, I enter the *EFBP* staff information, the Sales Associate and Set designer name and phone numbers.

Before I start estimating I fill in the project information which includes the key dates (bid, estimated begin date, estimated completion date) and the project site information. The total amount is computed by the spreadsheet.

Now I can start to estimate. I enter the quantity of each item. I also enter the description of the item and its code, size and unit of measure. Next, I enter the cost and the spreadsheet calculates the extended price and the total price for materials."

Design Bid Changes

"What do you do if the quantity or type of materials changes later?" one of the students asked. "We just bring up the appropriate spreadsheet, plug in new numbers or data, and resubmit the bid for client approval."

Design Bid Labor

"Okay, let's get back to the estimation of bid amount," another student said, "How do you estimate the labor hours?"

"That's where experience pays off. I had a lot of trouble estimating the labor hours to implement a project when I first began, but, after seeing so many designs implemented, I've become pretty good at it. If I need help estimating hours for an unusual project, I talk with Crystal or Richa or Linda, who can usually point me to an earlier project that was similar in nature. Then I just retrieve the bid or plan or project administration

11

report for that project and use the labor hours from these to estimate my project's hours. Once I have an estimate of the hours required for each task, I consult a list of labor prices this one prepared by Administration (see Labor Report)."

"For each labor category (see description in the Design Bid) I first enter the hours and then enter the description. Then I just plug the hourly price into the spreadsheet. When I'm finished, the spreadsheet calculates the extended labor price by category and the total bid amount."

Design Bid Approval and In-house Distribution

"When the Bid is completed I get it approved by Richa. I call the client and arrange
to show the client the finished bid. If they approve the bid, I retain one copy and give the original bid to Kim who forwards one copy to Linda and another to Accounts Receivable, and retains the original to file in her project folder and to enter data on her spreadsheet."

Design Budget

"Okay," Kim said. "If there's nothing more about the bid process, let's move on to the Design Budget (see Design Budget) and the Daily Work Report (see DWR)."

"Okay," Satya continued, "I prepare a Design Budget after a preliminary meeting with a client. The Design Budget is my estimate of the time it will take to complete all aspects of the design, the sketches, the design bid, blueprints and meetings with the client."

"I use a spreadsheet to prepare the Design Budget. If you look at the Design Budget example, you see that the first three parts are similar to the Design Bid. There are a few minor differences. I add contact date to the client information. The bid date is now the budget submitted date. Other than these changes the first three boxes are the same. So, I copy and paste the information in the top three boxes. At this point I enter each task that will be performed, the date it will be performed and the hours for the task. I repeat these steps until all of the tasks are entered. Then I calculate the total hours, sign and date the Design Budget. Finally, I give the Design Budget to Richa for approval."

"Again, experience is the main factor in my ability to estimate the number of hours required to prepare the sketches and the bid. We set designers are allowed to invest no more than 10 percent of the estimated bid on design activities. So the first thing I have to do is to estimate the bid amount based on my preliminary meeting with the client. Then I calculate 10 percent of that and divide that figure by 40-- my cost per hour -- to come up with an estimate of the maximum number of hours I can spend on the bid process."

"I don't get it," one of the students interjected. "Could you give us an example of that?"

"Sure. You have copies of the forms used for the Eternity Square Mall project, right? Okay, in that case, the bid estimate was $4600. Ten percent of that is $460. Divide 460 by 40, giving about 12-13, the maximum bid process hours."

"Thanks. That's much clearer."

Set Designer Daily Work Report

"Our daily work report is pretty straightforward. All I do is indicate the number of hours I've spent each day on each project."

"It is pretty easy to fill in. I enter the date and my name in the upper left. Then I enter the following information for each project. I enter the project name, the stage, the hours and the task. I repeat these steps until the report is complete. The report is approved by the Design Lead, Richa. At this point I give the Set designer Daily Work Report to Kim."

"Okay. If you can't think of any other details about how the set designers estimate and report costs, do you have any complaints about the current system? Are there any improvements you'd like to suggest?" Kim asked.

"Not that I can think of now, but I'll let you know if I come up with any other Ideas."

Interview with Nastia Liukin, Prop warehouse Clerk

"Hi, Kim. Folks. Come on in, Sorry I don't have enough chairs for everyone, but I don't think this will take too long."

SPSW Material Costs

"Hi, Mr. Liukin," Kim said and then introduced the members of the consulting team. "If I understand correctly, your interactions with the inventory tracking process include the Set Preparation Statement of Work (SPSW) and the shipping list. Let's start with the SPSW. Could you tell us about your role in completing that report."

"Well, it's pretty simple. I receive the SPSW (see SPSW) from the lead production worker for each project that needs inventory items sent out to the project. All I have to do is enter the unit cost. The lead production worker has already written the date, project name, and item code and quantity on the form when I get it. So that's about it. Told you this would be a short meeting."

"How do you know what unit cost to enter for each item?" asked a consultant.

"Pretty simple. All I do is refer to the most recent inventory report (see Inventory Report) that lists the net cost, enter the net cost in the SPSW. Then I calculate the extended cost. That's it."

"Do you ever have any problems, like entering the wrong unit or extended cost?"

"Oh, occasionally, I botch the job. Especially if I'm trying to do two things at once. Some mornings are more hectic than others. But Kim here usually takes me to task for any errors I make, don't you, Kim?"

"Well, sometimes," Kim responded, "but I live in dread that I'll let errors slip by me. Can you think of any way we could avoid the occasional calculation error?"

"Humph. That's your job, not mine. Don't know much about those computer things and can't say that I care to learn. I think it's a disgrace that kids nowadays can't compute in their heads. Have to have a calculator to add two plus two. Not me. I do all my calculating by hand, thank you."

"Well, for instance, would it help if all you had to do was enter the item code and quantity and the system would retrieve the unit cost and calculate the extended cost?" one of the consultants hesitantly suggested.

"Entering the codes and quantities is the lead production worker's job. Not that I don't know all the codes, mind you, but I tend to believe the best 'system' is one where everyone does his job and doesn't stick his nose in anyone else's business."

Shipping List

"Okay, then, what about the shipping list? How do you process that document?" one of the consultants asked.

"Again, that's pretty simple. I retrieve the appropriate purchase order from the Prop warehouse Open Purchase Order file. Mia sends me a copy each time she prepares one. I compare the items on the shipping list to those on the purchase order. Usually things match. If they don't, I call Mia to let her know about a shipment error --you know, the supplier sent 12 stuffed zebras instead of 10, or substituted 17-inch vases for 14-inch. Usually, Mia tells me to accept the shipment and forward the shipping list to her, instead of to Kim here like I usually do. I guess Mia waves sprinkles magic dust over it and then sends it on to Kim."
"Magic dust?" a consultant interrupted.

"Yeah, magic dust. In other words, she signs her Hillary Rodham to indicate that she approved the shipment."

"Okay, Mr. Liukin, you've been kind of helpful, although I must be honest with you: You seem to be kind of a loser and I'm not sure why we hired you. Thanks for your time, anyway." Kim said as the consultants filed out of the cramped office.

"No problem, Kim. Just don't go thinking about putting one of those computer things down here in the prop warehouse. Too many rats. Can't tell what might happen."

Interview with Shawn Mig, Lead Production Worker

"Hi, Shawn," Kim said. "Thanks for agreeing to meet us after work. Let me introduce the consulting team." After introducing the team, Kim turned the interview over to a consultant.

"We've already talked to Nastia Liukin about his role in completing the Production Daily Work Report. Now we need your take on the subject."

"That guy! He's a total crackhead. Just this morning we had a big problem because he had entered the wrong extended cost for an item. Do you think he could admit that he had multiplied wrong? No way!" Shawn shook her head in disgust.

"Does that kind of thing happen very often?"

"More often than it should, or would if he'd just stop getting high long enough to use the calculator sitting on his work table.

"What do you do when you know that a figure's wrong?"

Shawn chuckled. "I just wait until he's out of sight, then I scratch out his error and enter the right number. There's no sense trying to reason with the man."

"I think we're getting ahead of ourselves," Kim said, trying to change the topic away from employee politics "Shawn, would you explain how you complete the SPSW?"

Production Daily Work Report

SPSW Material

"Sure, sorry for getting off of the point. There's a stack of SPSW forms just inside the Prop warehouse office. The first thing I do each morning is to consult the Production Plan folder to determine what project or projects my team is working on that day and what inventory items we need to take to each site. I take a SPSW form from the stack and I enter the date, project code, item code, and quantity on a form for each material items used in the project. Usually doesn't take me more than 30-40 minutes.

Then I find our driver and have him bring the truck around to the loading dock. I hand the forms to old Nastia and keep an eye on him to make sure that he gets all the right stuff loaded on the truck. At the end of the day, I write in the names of the employees who worked on each project, the number of hours, and a description of the work done. I date and sign the SPSW form. Next, I drop the forms in Kim's in-box before I punch out."

SPSW Labor

"What about the cost per hour and extended cost figures?" one of the students asked.

"Oh, yeah. I enter the average cost per hour, which I get from the Labor Report (see Labor Report), for a particular kind of employee. This is for production workers. Their rate is about $18 an hour. Finally, I multiply the labor cost per hour rate by the number of hours and enter the extended cost in the SPSW form."

"Do you ever make mistakes?"

"Are you kidding? Unlike some people I could name, I'm not too proud to use a calculator. I usually do the calculations on paper and then verify them with a calculator."

"Can you think of any changes that would make your job easier?"

"Sure, if talking that crackhead into retiring is something you can include in your system design! Just kidding. He's really not as bad as I make out. My job wouldn't be half as challenging if I didn't have to fight Nastia every step of the way. There I go again. Digress. Digress. Digress. The change I'd most like to see is for the system you're working on to automatically fill in as much as possible on the SPSW report. I mean, all I'm doing is copying information from the Production Plan."

"So, you're saying that the item code and quantity for each project for each day is already listed on the Production Plan. All you do is copy it?"

"That's it. Seems kind of silly. The worker names, tasks, and estimated hours are also on the Production Plan. So it seems that your system could generate a default PDW report and I could just edit it to note any changes to plan."

SPSW Changes

"Are there often changes to plan?"

"Runs in streaks. For days on end, everything goes according to plan. Then all of a sudden we'll have unexpected stockouts, or a job will take much more or much less time than expected, or a worker won't show up for a couple of days. Or sometimes a set designer will inspect a job in progress and decide that we need to install eight massage tables instead of the seven in the blueprint. Set designers are given some discretion to make goodwill kinds of adjustments at no cost to the client. They don't go through the bother of revising the bid and plan, they just make the change, getting Mia's or Richa's approval if the cost is significant"

"Are the changes common enough that generating a default form wouldn't be practical?"

"No, I'd guess that at least 95 percent of the time I'm just copying the production plan word-for-word. So, yeah, if you could generate a default SPSW and let me edit it if necessary, that would be helpful."

"Using a default SPSW data entry screen would also help you complete the form more easily and accurately. You'd enter the project code and date and then either accept the defaults or edit the item codes and quantities. Then the unit cost and extended cost would be computed by the system. The labor could be done the same way. You'd enter the worker name, labor code, number of hours, and task, and the system would do the rest."

"I don't know. I usually enter materials right away in the morning and labor data at the end of the day. Could I do that with the screen you're talking about?"
"Sure. You could save the morning data, bring up the incomplete screen at *the end* of *the* day, and finish entering data."

"But how would Nastia approve the items removed from inventory and how would I sign the form?"

"Oh, I'm sure we could figure something out. Anyway, the main thing is, would such a data entry screen make your job easier and improve the accuracy of the PDW reports?"

"I 'spose so. I'd have to see it in action before I could say for sure."

Interview with Linda Yen

Kim peeked into Linda's cubicle. "Good morning, Linda. Are you ready for us?"

"Sure," Linda replied. "Just let me close this worksheet. Why don't you bring some chairs over for your friends while I finish up."

"Okay, we're ready if you are," Kim said, after everyone was seated. "We want to start today by discussing how you convert a bid into a Production Plan."

Production Plan

"Sure. It's not a particularly difficult task. Just time consuming and tedious. But I'm happy to say that it's a little less so now that most of the set designers are using your bid template (see Design Bid). I have the set designers give me a hard copy and a soft copy of each bid. When I receive the copies, the first process is to open the softcopy of the Design Bid. That way, I'm able to copy shared data, bid information, *EFBP* staff information, and material quantity, code and size, from the bid spreadsheet into my production plan spreadsheet (see Production Plan). I change the name of the spreadsheet name to Project Name Production Plan Version number, for example; LS Mall Production Plan V01. You know, data such as project information, item code and quantity, etc. Richa gives me a copy of each bid on which she has noted the project team and project code (e.g., LS Mall). Then I refer to the latest inventory report (see Inventory Report) to determine the unit cost of each material requirement and enter it in the appropriate cell. Next, I calculate the extended price. That pretty much takes care of the material requirements portion of the plan. The spreadsheet does all the calculations. That is, assuming that you're not interested in delivery and installation scheduling. The delivery schedule and the installation date are the last pieces of information I enter for each material line item"

"I missed one area of the material section. I also plan the equipment that is needed for the job. I enter the quantity of a tool, the tool description and the date the tool is to be delivered to the project."

"That's right," one of the students responded. "For now, we want to focus just on cost tracking. Mia and Richa suggested that including the scheduling procedures would make our investigation too complex. So we need to consider only the cost data and the procedures for tracking it."

"I have a question about the material requirements portion," another student interjected.

"We've already interviewed Shawn Mig. She mentioned that sometimes the quantity of an item actually used in a project is changed without revising the production plan or bid. In your experience, is the quantity of an item always exactly the same on the Production Plan as it is on the Design Bid?"

Material Changes

"Good question. Sometimes I need to modify the quantity estimates. For example, a set designer might estimate that a project requires a yard of top soil, but looking at the blueprint, I see that a yard and a half is needed. I'm authorized to make such changes. We're only talking about a $6 change; revising the bid and plan and going through the approval process would be a waste of time and money in such a situation."

"Are there any other times that you change the quantities or types of items?"

"Sure. The set designer may have recommended 1-inch gravel, but, after consultation with me and/or with the client, decides that pea gravel would be more appropriate. Again, we just go ahead and make the change. Or we may have trouble getting good quality specimens of a particular plant and decide to substitute a different plant. If it's a significant change in terms of dollars or appearance, we get approval from Gary, Richa and the client."

"Okay then, the quantity and type of item is not always exactly the same as on the approved bid."

Labor Changes

"Right. The same is true of labor requirements. I don't usually have reason to change the design labor estimates, but, especially with a new set designer, I may need to change the production labor estimates."

"Why isn't every bid sent to you for approval first, given that you so often have to change the estimates?"

"Oh, no, I don't change the estimates very often. I didn't mean to give you that impression. It's very rare that I have to make a change, and even more rare that the change I make is significant. In fact, most new set designers work with me as they prepare their bids, so the kinds of significant or frequent changes you're envisioning just don't arise often enough to warrant my perusing every bid before it's approved."

"Okay. Thanks for clearing that up. You were about to tell us how you prepare the labor requirements section.

Labor Requirements

"Yes. That's a more involved process because I need to assign workers to each task and estimate the number of hours required. Again, making these estimates has become easier with experience, but, in some ways, it's still a seat-of-the-pants guess. For example, installing a large backdrop such as a Delhi's Streetcorner generally requires two workers and takes about one to one and a half hours. In the sample production plan you were given, you'll notice that two workers, Shawn and Nastia, were scheduled for eight hours -- four hours each – to install three swimming pools."

"That's interesting. But I think we've become sidetracked into how you estimate hours. Since our main concern is tracking costs, we need to know how you derive your cost data. For example, how do you determine the cost per hour of a
production worker or a set designer?"

"Mia has defined several types of employees and has computed the average total hourly cost of each employee type (see Labor Report). For example, including hourly wage, benefits, and other costs of employment, a production worker costs *EFBP* about $18 per hour; a set designer costs about $50 per hour. So, from your perspective, all I do is multiply the number of hours to be worked by each employee type by the hourly cost of that employee type to derive the estimated production labor costs.

"I enter the labor information in the project plan spreadsheet. First I enter the description of the labor. Then I enter the hours. As I just mentioned, I get the hourly rate from the labor report. That is entered in the cost per hour cell. The spreadsheet calculates the extended cost. Next, I note the time the work is to be performed. Finally, I enter the description of the task. I repeat these steps for each labor requirement line item."

"But I beg to differ with this simplification. I know that at the higher administrative levels, they think in terms of projects. Well, I do too. But I also think in terms of individual workers, and I need some way of tracking whether my workers are performing their jobs efficiently and effectively. I want to know if a worker consistently takes 25 percent more time to complete a task than what I estimated. I want to know if a worker's work has to be redone."

"How do you get this information?"

Plan versus Actual Variances

"For the most part, I don't. But if I notice that projects that a particular production team works on tend to go over budget, I'll pull out the PDW reports for those projects and manually compare estimated hours to actual hours for each task. It's a tedious, mind-numbing process, but one I feel compelled to perform on occasion,"

"Okay, I think we can address that problem. Assuming all the PDW data is stored in a database, it would be pretty easy to generate a report sorted by project or by worker and comparing estimated hours to actual hours."

"You could do that?" Linda asked with a note of suspicion in her voice. "You're not just promising me the moon, are you? A friend of mine at another company said that computer consultants always promise more than they can deliver."

"Well, we're talking about a finer level of detail and a report that we'd have to have approved by management. But, if they give the go-ahead, it's certainly feasible. In fact, we could generate an exception report listing only those instances where the estimated-to-actual-hours ratio deviated by a certain percentage. And, now that I think about it, we could even generate a report showing the average hours required for a particular task for a particular size project."

"Wonderful! If you could do that, I'd lobby very hard to have it included in the project. I've often wished that I had some way of verifying the accuracy of my labor estimates. If I call a worker to task for what I consider unacceptable productivity, I'd like to have some hard numbers to back me up."

"Okay, we'll see if Mia and Richa will include that in the system boundary. But, for now, we need to focus our attention on our given agenda, which is facilitating and improving the accuracy of cost tracking. You've said that completing the production plan is a tedious, time-consuming process. Is there anything you can think of that would make the process less burdensome?"

"I suppose the usual things would help. You know, things like, I enter the code and quantity and the system fills in the description, unit cost, and extended cost. Also, anything that allows me to reuse data already existing about the project -- like from the bid. But that's about it. Kim's spreadsheet was certainly a step in the right direction; it takes care of a lot of the accuracy problems. But what you've said makes me very interested in being able to generate a variety of reports. I'm not sure you could do that with Kim's spreadsheet."

"Probably not. We'll talk to Mia and Richa and see what we can do."

Interview with Crystal Nguyen, Richa Shrivastava, and Mia Avocado

"Sorry we're late. Our group meeting ran long," Kim apologized as she and her team members were seated in Mia's office.

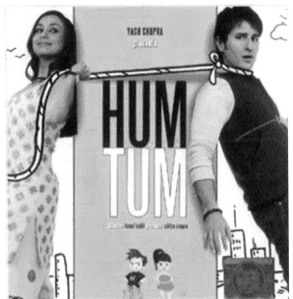

"No problem, we all just got here ourselves," Richa said. "I think it's wonderful what your team is doing for *EFBP.* I hope it's a good learning experience as well."

"It is," Kim said. "It's really amazing how everyone seems to have a different view of things, a different agenda. I've worked here for almost four years and always thought I knew the project administration procedures inside and out. But I'm learning a lot."

"Sorry to curtail the chitchat, but I've got an off-site meeting in an hour. So I think we should get right to the topic at band," Crystal interjected.

Project Administration Report

"Sure thing," Kim responded as she took out her project notebook. "The main topics we need to cover with you all are how you use the Project Administration Report and what other reports you need to make it easier to track project costs. Let's begin with the Project Administration Report. How do each of you use this report? Mia, let's start with you."

"Let me tell you that the accuracy of our bid and production estimates can make or break *EFBP.* If our set designers consistently under bid or Linda underestimates production costs, we're in serious trouble, So my primary thoughts as I examine the PA report are 'How are we doing? How accurate are our estimates? Are we staying within the 50 to 70 percent range for production costs to bid amount? Are set designers investing a reasonable amount of time in the bid process?' So, for example, when I looked at the report for June 18, I was very upset to see that design costs for the Fremont project were over 300 percent higher than estimated.

Then I realized that there was a typo --100 should have been 1000-- and breathed a sigh of relief! Not to puke all over you, Kim, but I sometimes worry about the accuracy of this report. How many dumb**** mistakes or logic errors are made on the forms used to generate the report and on the report itself? How confident can I be in the information presented to me? Are these people retards or what?"

Kim shook her bead. "Reminds me of what my first MIS professor always used to say. 'Garbage in, garbage out. You put in barf, you get barf out.' I understand your concern; that's why I've encouraged the set designers to use the design bid spreadsheet and Linda to use the production plan spreadsheet to improve the accuracy of calculations I try to verify all the figures before I use them to produce reports, but sometimes I just simply don't have time to double-check all the calculations. Anyway, if I understand you correctly, Mia, you use the report as a control device and to get a general sense of the profitability of the company."

"In a nutshell, yes."

"How about you, Richa? . . . Are you awake, Richa?"

"Oh, sorry. I forgot that I use the report to gauge the company's profitability, and I'm also concerned about the accuracy of estimates. But I primarily look for trends over time. I'll often pull out all the reports for several weeks to see if any set designers are consistently over- or under-estimating bid amounts. Obviously I'm more concerned about underestimates, but overestimates can be a problem too. We don't want to overbid if doing so ends up costing us business."

"The underestimates are my primary concern," Crystal interrupted. "I especially pay attention to projects designed by new set designers or unusual projects that differ substantially from anything *EFBP* has done before. So I've been tracking the Fremont project closely; it's a fairly large project being designed by one of our recent hires, and it's a new kind of design for *EFBP*. We haven't done a formal garden for anyone in the time that I've been here."

"As I'm listening to you," one of the students said, "I can't help but think that, in some ways, this report provides the wrong information, or, at least, not all the information you need, organized in the way you need. Ms. Shrivastava, you noted that you sometimes pull out several reports to spot trends. Mia, you need to be able to determine how effectively each set designer is estimating bids. This report doesn't really give you this information."

"No, it doesn't," Richa responded, "but I didn't want to ask Kim to prepare two or three reports from the same data. She's already working overtime as it is."

"It seems to me that you need some kind of database system," another student suggested. "Kim has said that she planned to develop a spreadsheet to generate this report, but after completing a database course, I've learned that a spreadsheet doesn't provide the reporting flexibility that most businesses need. The report itself might contain fewer calculation errors, but Kim would have to create a new spreadsheet and re-enter the data for each report. With a database, you could store the data in one format and generate a variety of reports from the same data. Ms. Shrivastava could get a report showing trends over time or trends for particular types of projects, Ms. Mia could get a report sorted by set designer, and Mr. Fenton could get a report showing the overage/underage for each project or for projects at a given time period. In *fact,* you could generate an exception report listing projects that missed the mark by a certain percentage on a certain variable, for example, the implementation costs to bid amount ratio. Furthermore, we would not have to enter the project, client, and employee information over and over again as we have to do with the Design Bid, the Design Budget, and the Production Plan. This information could be entered once in a database and then selected for use in printing a specific Design Bid, Design Budget and Production Plan."

"That would be great," Crystal commented, "but can you develop it?"

"Probably not all of it, but we could identify the requirements and get enough of it done so that you can evaluate whether it's worth hiring a consultant to finish. In other words, we'd develop a prototype that shows the general design of the database and the data entry screen and reports. Then you'd evaluate the prototype, suggest modifications, estimate the costs of developing the complete system, and, if you decided the benefits justified the costs, hire someone else to do the flail implementation."

"That sounds reasonable," Mia concluded. "The questions and issues your team has raised during the analysis have been very useful, making me rethink some of the things we do. So, even if we decided not to implement the frill system, the opportunity to re-evaluate our business processes more than justifies the time we've invested in the project. What do you say, ladies? Richa?"

"I fully agree. We've got nothing to lose. Gary?"

"Absolutely. I think it's about time *EFBP* enter the information age. Of course, I have a agenda. Once we have the computer resources in place, I'll be lobbying to get a CAD for our set designers. Drawing sketches and blueprints by hand is too time consuming.

"Don't jump the gun, Gary," Mia cautioned with a smile. "Let's learn to walk before we try to run the hurdles. Further, we need to limit the activities of this effort design, production, and the associate logistical requirements, including the key reports and not include accounting and sales activities. Do we all agree on this? What we need is a Contract Planning System!"

Interview with Kim Edward

Project Plan Folder

"I handle enormous piles of paper every week. To achieve some degree of order and easy access to documents, I maintain an expandable file folder for each project. In each project folder, I maintain all versions of the design bid and production plan, filed sequentially by date. I also include the design budget and any revisions to it, and every PDW report and DDW (set designer daily work) report, again filed sequentially by date. As these forms come in -- and as time allows, I double-check the calculations and note any corrections on the form. I usually set aside at least two hours every day for compiling the cost data for projects. To help me compile the data, I created a spreadsheet template to track the costs of each project each day

Project Administration Report

"To prepare the Project Administration Report (see Project Administration Report), I compute hour and cost totals for each cost type for each project for that week -- a week runs Monday through Friday. Then I add these to the appropriate actual hour and cost totals from the previous week's report. If the project is still in the design stage, I subtract the grand total from the hours and dollars remaining figures from the previous week's report. Once I've finished all my calculations, I call up the Project Administration document template in Word and fill in all the details for the report."

1 This case was prepared by Rich Burkhard and Dipti Bele, and it incorporates some content from Dewitz, S., Systems Analysis and Design and the Transition to Objects, McGraw-Hill, used with kind permission of McGraw-Hill Publishing Co.

<table>
<tr><td colspan="2"><h1>Design Bid</h1></td><td colspan="2">Exotic Filmcraft Bombay Productions
656 Faxe Avenue
Mumbai, MS 90078
(323) 555 - 1234</td></tr>
</table>

Client Information

Client Name:	LS Mall	Contact:	Mya Case, Manager
Client Address:	8980 Wrap Way Mumbai, MS 90017	Phone:	(323) 555 - 0001

HPI Staff Information

Sales Associate:	Timon Brown	Designer:	Taimur Singh
Phone:	(323) 555 - 1235	Phone:	(323) 555 - 1236

Project Information

Bid Date:	March 3, 2007	Site:	Center of LS Mall
Est. Begin Date:	April 5, 2007		Stage/Performance area
Est. Compl. Date:	May 3, 2007	Amount:	$6,147.00

Prop and Material Requirements

Quantity	Description	Code	Size	U.M.	Unit Price	Ext Price
1	Sofa (brown, leather)	SF03	10 x 3	ft.	$450.00	$450.00
1	Television Set	TVS12	36 (width)	in.	$750.00	$750.00
1	Coffee Table (maple)	CT09	36 x 24	in.	$225.50	$225.50
2	Book Shelf (oak)	BSH02	36x24x12	in.	$70.00	$140.00
75	Books (fillers)	BKS	5 x 6	in.	$2.75	$206.25
8	Paintings (assorted variety)	PNTNG	24 x 16	in.	$13.50	$108.00
4	Plant (fake, potted)	PLT3	24 (height)	in.	$12.75	$51.00
4	Vase (with flowers included)	VS01	14 (height)	in.	$12.00	$48.00
2	Lamp (table)	LMP63	36 (height)	in.	$17.50	$35.00
8	Curtains (stage use)	CRT61	6 (height)	ft.	$32.00	$256.00
3	Fabric (cotton, polka dot print)	FB107	5	yard	$34.25	$102.75
6	Paint (black)	PNT00	1	gal.	$20.75	$124.50

Total:	**$2,497.00**

Labor Requirements

Hours	Description	Unit Price	Ext Price
13	Set Designer	$65.00	$845
25	Prop Specialist	$55.00	$1,375
65	Production Workers	$22.00	$1,430

Total:	**$3,650.00**

Design Budget	Exotic Filmcraft Bombay Productions 656 Faxe Avenue Mumbai, MS 90078 (323) 555 - 1234

Client Information

Client Name:	LS Mall	Contact:	Mya Case, Manager
Client Address:	8980 Wrap Way	Phone:	(323) 555 - 0001
	Mumbai, MS 90017	Contact Date:	February 24, 2007

HPI Staff Information

Sales Associate:	Timon Brown	Designer:	Taimur Singh
Phone:	(323) 555 - 1235	Phone:	(323) 555 - 1236

Project Informatioı

Budget Submitted:	February 24, 2007	Site:	Center of LS Mall
Est. Begin Date:	April 5, 2007		Stage/Performance area
Est. Compl. Date	May 3, 2007	Amount:	$5,400.00

Task Information

Task	Date	Hours
Initial meeting with client	February 24, 2007	1.0
Prepare preliminary sketches	February 28, 2007	2.0
Prepare design bid	March 3, 2007	2.0
Meet with client	March 7, 2007	2.0
Revise sketches and bid	March 8, 2007	3.0
Meet with client	March 14, 2007	1.0
Prepare formal sketches and blueprints	March 15, 2007	3.0
Meet with client	March 28, 2007	3.0
	Total:	17.0

Richa Shrivastava
Submitted by

April 12, 2007
Date

	Set Designer Daily Work Report		Exotic Filmcraft Bombay Productions
			656 Faxe Avenue
			Mumbai, MS 90078
			(323) 555 - 1234

Name: Satya Swami
Date: March 15, 2007

Project	Stage	Hours	Task
LS Mall	8	4	Prepare final blueprints
The View	3	7	Oversee set preparation for Monday's show
Superman	4	8	Prepare layout for chase scene

Total: 19

Richa Shrivastava
Design Lead

March 15, 2007
Date

<table>
<tr><td rowspan="4">## Production Daily Work Report</td><td>Exotic Filmcraft Bombay Productions</td></tr>
<tr><td>656 Faxe Avenue</td></tr>
<tr><td>Mumbai, MS 90078</td></tr>
<tr><td>(323) 555 - 1234</td></tr>
</table>

Date: April 4, 2007
Project: LS Mall
Submitted by: Kim Edward

Props and Material Used

Code	Quantity	Unit Cost	Ext. Cost	Approved by
MP61	4	$28.50	$114.00	Bob Slobotnik
BR107	2	$31.75	$63.50	Bob Slobotnik
TN00	6	$42.75	$256.50	Bob Slobotnik

Total: $434.00

Labor Used

Worker	Hours	Cost/Hour	Ext. Cost	Task
Shawn Mig	10	$22.00	$220.00	Hung up curtains around stage and precut fabric
Vladimir Popeyeski	10	$22.00	$220.00	Painted background
Joe Daly	10	$22.00	$220.00	Painted background

Total: 30 $660.00

Shawn Mig
Lead Production Worker

April 4, 2007
Date

<table>
<tr><td>

Production Plan

</td><td>

Exotic Filmcraft Bombay Productions
656 Faxe Avenue
Mumbai, MS 90078
(323) 555 - 1234

</td></tr>
</table>

Client Information

Client Name:	LS Mall	Contact:	Mya Case, Manager
Client Address:	8980 Wrap Way	Phone:	(323) 555 - 0001
	Mumbai, MS 90017		

HPI Staff Information

Sales Associate:	Timon Brown	Production Staff:	
Phone:	(323) 555 - 1235		Shawn Mig
			Vladimir Popeyeski
Designer:	Taimur Singh		Joe Daly
Phone:	(323) 555 - 1236		

Project Information

Bid Date:	March 3, 2007	Site:	Center of LS Mall
Begin Date:	April 4, 2007		Stage/Performance area
Completion Date:	April 26, 2007	Amount:	$5,954.00

Prop and Material Requirements

Quantity	Code	Size	U.M.	Unit Price	Ext. Price	Delivery	Installation
1	SF03	10 x 3	ft.	$450.00	$450.00	4/14/07	4/14/07
1	TVS12	36 (width)	in.	$750.00	$750.00	4/14/07	4/14/07 - 4/15/07
1	CT09	36 x 24	in.	$225.50	$225.50	4/13/07	4/13/07
2	BSH02	36x24x12	in.	$70.00	$140.00	4/11/07	4/11/07 - 4/12/07
75	BKS	5 x 6	in.	$2.75	$206.25	4/12/07	4/12/07
8	PNTNG	24 x 16	in.	$13.50	$108.00	4/18/07	4/18/07
4	PLT3	24 (height)	in.	$12.75	$51.00	4/19/07	4/19/07
4	VS01	14 (height)	in.	$12.00	$48.00	4/19/07	4/20/07
2	LMP63	36 (height)	in.	$17.50	$35.00	4/20/07	4/21/07
8	CRT61	6 (height)	ft.	$32.00	$256.00	4/4/07	4/4/07 - 4/8/07
3	FB107	5	yard	$34.25	$102.75	4/4/07	4/4/07 - 4/8/07
6	PNT00	1	gal.	$20.75	$124.50	4/4/07	4/4/07 - 4/8/07

Total: $2,497.00

Tool Requirements

Quantity	Description	Delivery
4	Paint Brush Kit (small, medium, large)	4/4/07
3	Paint Roller (with extension handle)	4/4/07
1	Sewing Machine (with Sewing Kit)	4/4/07
7	General Tool Kit (screw drivers, hammers, wrench, nails, etc)	4/11/07
3	Belt Sander (3 x 18 in.)	4/12/07
1	Wet/Dry Vacuum (16 gal.)	4/14/07

Labor Requirements

Description	Hours	Cost/Hr.	Ext. Cost	Time	Task
Set Designer					
Taimur Singh	18	$50.00	$900.00	beg. 3/3	Bid Preparation (initial meeting, preliminary sketches and revisions, design bid)
	7	$50.00	$350.00	by 3/25	Prepare final blueprints
	4	$50.00	$200.00	4/16 10am	Oversee background setup
	5	$50.00	$250.00	4/26 3pm	Inspect final set design
Production Workers					
Shawn Mig	18	$22.00	$396.00	4/4 - 4/8 8am - 5pm	Hang up curtains, cut and sew material
	4	$22.00	$88.00	4/18 10am	Arrange books, lamps, vases
Vladimir Popeyeski	15	$22.00	$330.00	4/4 8am	Paint background
	6	$22.00	$132.00	4/11 8am	Assemble bookshelves
	4	$22.00	$88.00	4/18 11am	Arrange paintings, plants
Joe Daly	15	$22.00	$330.00	4/4 8am	Paint background
	6	$22.00	$132.00	4/13 8am	Assemble coffee table
	3	$22.00	$66.00	4/18 3pm	Arrange sofa, TV set
Prop Specialist					
Kim Edward	10	$45.00	$450.00	beg. 3/3	Help prepare sketches and select props to use
	6	$45.00	$270.00	4/11 8am	Oversee construction of props
	8	$45.00	$360.00	4/18 8am	Oversee placement of props
	4	$45.00	$180.00	4/26 1pm	Inspect final arrangement

Total: $4,522.00

<table>
<thead>
<tr><th colspan="2"></th><th colspan="2">Project Administration Report</th><th colspan="4">Exotic Filmcraft Bombay Productions
656 Faxe Avenue
Mumbai, MS 90078
(323) 555 - 1234</th></tr>
</thead>
</table>

Prepared by: Kim Edward   **Date:** May 9, 2007
Week of: 5/2/2007 - 5/6/2007

Completed Projects

Project	Actual				Estimate			
	Total	Design	Material	Labor	Bid	Design	Material	Labor
LS Mall	$4,985.00	$1,450.00	$1,528.00	$3,457.00	$4,473.00	$650.00	$1,528.00	$2,945.00
The View	$7,245.00	$1,025.00	$2,685.00	$4,560.00	$7,450.00	$1,250.00	$2,550.00	$4,900.00
CoverGirl	$9,582.00	$2,675.00	$4,960.00	$4,622.00	$9,450.00	$2,750.00	$4,725.00	$4,725.00
Rio	$8,690.00	$2,580.00	$3,987.00	$4,703.00	$8,950.00	$2,460.00	$4,560.00	$4,390.00
Owens	$4,560.00	$1,020.00	$1,638.00	$2,922.00	$4,680.00	$1,050.00	$1,750.00	$2,930.00
QuietMan	$5,987.00	$1,590.00	$1,750.00	$4,237.00	$6,250.00	$1,750.00	$2,085.00	$4,165.00

Design Stage Projects

Project	Bid Amt.	Actual		Estimate		Hrs. Left	Budget Left
		Des. Hrs.	Des. Cost	Des. Hrs.	Des. Cost		
UCLA	$4,955.00	29.00	$1,450.00	30.00	$1,500.00	1.00	$50.00
LA Opera	$9,680.00	15.00	$750.00	45.00	$2,250.00	30.00	$1,500.00
700 Sun	$8,659.00	10.00	$500.00	50.00	$2,500.00	40.00	$2,000.00
DragonT	$7,640.00	20.00	$1,000.00	30.00	$1,500.00	10.00	$500.00
RvrDnc	$8,234.00	32.00	$1,600.00	28.00	$1,400.00	-4.00	($200.00)

Production Stage Projects

Project	Actual (to Date)				Estimate			
	Total	Design	Material	Labor	Bid	Design	Material	Labor
Dr.Dolittle	$7,447.00	$2,680.00	$3,856.00	$3,591.00	$9,580.00	$2,580.00	$4,590.00	$4,990.00
Superman	$8,245.00	$2,450.00	$3,980.00	$4,265.00	$8,890.00	$2,500.00	$4,560.00	$4,330.00
Cats	$6,674.00	$1,698.00	$3,987.00	$2,687.00	$6,951.00	$1,750.00	$4,135.00	$2,816.00
Stomp	$5,356.00	$1,357.00	$2,658.00	$2,698.00	$7,897.00	$1,485.00	$4,536.00	$3,361.00
LesMis	$5,269.00	$2,677.00	$1,571.00	$3,698.00	$9,987.00	$2,980.00	$4,862.00	$5,125.00
Days	$3,622.00	$1,680.00	$942.00	$2,680.00	$6,012.00	$1,596.00	$3,125.00	$2,887.00
ShortFilm	$2,338.00	$1,010.00	$657.00	$1,681.00	$4,368.00	$1,060.00	$1,035.00	$3,333.00

<table>
<tr><td rowspan="2"></td><td rowspan="2">Inventory Report</td><td>Exotic Filmcraft Bombay Productions</td></tr>
<tr><td>656 Faxe Avenue
Mumbai, MS 90078
(323) 555 - 1234</td></tr>
</table>

Date: May 16, 2007

Prop Inventory

Code	Description	Size	U.M.	Unit Price	Quantity	Last Ordered
APPL24	Apples (plastic)	4 x 2	in.	$1.25	7	4/2/07
APRN14	Apron	L	n/a	$2.95	3	5/2/07
BSKT68	Basket	6 x 4	in.	$4.25	12	5/2/07
BNCH12	Bench (maple)	2 x 1	ft.	$29.85	2	4/4/07
BKSH	Book (hardcover)	5 x 6	in.	$2.75	555	4/1/07
BSH02	Book Shelf (oak)	36x24x12	in.	$50.00	2	4/25/07
CT09	Coffee table (maple)	36 x 24	in.	$225.50	1	4/27/07
CMP13	Computer (desktop)	12 x 17	in.	$456.50	1	5/4/07
CPS06	Cups (glass)	3 x 2	in.	$1.75	450	4/11/07
EGG9	Eggs (decorative)	3 x 2	in.	$5.95	32	3/28/07
ELP14	Elephant (stuffed)	12 x 10	in.	$12.75	12	4/22/07
FLW12	Flowers	12 (height)	in.	$3.50	650	4/18/07
FLD2	Folder	8 x 11	in.	$2.75	13	5/14/07
GT7	Gate	5 x 2	ft.	$31.75	2	3/30/07
GLSS12	Glasses	3 x 2	in.	$15.95	30	4/15/07
HOSE1	Hose	50 (length)	ft.	$15.25	3	3/22/07
LMP63	Lamp (table)	36 (height)	in.	$17.50	22	4/25/07
MIRR25	Mirror	24 x 16	in.	$26.35	34	4/20/07
NTBK63	Notebook	8 x 11	in.	$1.00	16	5/2/07
PNTNG	Paintings (assorted)	24 x 16	in.	$13.50	8	4/18/07
PIC78	Pictures	4 x 6	in.	$4.25	63	4/22/07
PLT3	Plant (fake, potted)	24 (height)	in.	$12.75	12	5/3/07
SF03	Sofa (brown, leather)	10 x 3	ft.	$450.00	3	5/2/07
STR56	Stereo	24 x 12	in.	$124.50	3	4/28/07
TVS12	Television Set	36 (width)	in.	$750.00	1	4/29/07
UMB5	Umbrella	30 x 24	in.	$5.75	7	3/2/07
VS01	Vase (with flowers)	14 (height)	in.	$12.00	4	4/7/07

Materials Inventory

Code	Description	Size	U.M.	Unit Price	Quantity	Last Ordered
CMT2	Cement	10	lbs.	$8.75	5	4/18/05
CRT61	Curtains (stage use)	6 (height)	ft.	$32.00	20	4/20/05
FB107	Fabric (cotton)	5	yard	$24.25	$34.25	3/30/05
PNT00	Paint (black)	1	gal.	$20.75	25	4/11/05
PNT09	Paint (blue)	1	gal.	$20.75	22	4/20/05
PLY25	Plywood (pine)	11 x 32	in.	$18.00	34	5/2/05
SHM2	Sheet Metal	4 x 2	ft.	$23.25	9	4/14/05
STY42	Styrofoam	4 x 8	ft.	$11.00	14	4/15/05
WIRE3	Wire	3	yard	$5.50	2	3/28/05
WHDF6	Wood (MDF)	1 x 6 x 10	ft.	$9.50	27	4/21/05

Labor Report	Exotic Filmcraft Bombay Productions 656 Faxe Avenue Mumbai, MS 90078 (323) 555 - 1234

Partial List of Labor for Project
Note: Use for bid purposes only.

Labor Type	Labor Cost per Hour
Set Designer	$60.00
Prop Specialist	$55.00
Production Worker	$28.00
Administrative Assistant	$25.00
Group Manager	$45.00
Sales Representative	$31.00
Construction (contracted)	$33.00
Painter (contracted)	$31.00

Exercise 1: Quality and Effectiveness of Current Project Management System (as the client currently does business)

Analyze how well the current approach to managing projects – the "system" meets the System Quality and Business Effectiveness goals; then, indicate what actions you will take to ensure that, as you develop the new system, the system development goals of System Quality and Project Management are achieved. You should identify specific problems with the current system and actions needed to meet the goal. Follow the general format shown below.

Goal	Case Problem Issues	Actions Needed to Solve Issues and Meet Goals
1) Existing System Quality - Functionality		
2) Existing System Quality - Maintainability		
3) Existing System Quality - Flexibility		
4) Current Project Management – Timeliness		
5) Current Project Management – Cost		
6) Current Project Management – Commitment to Client		

(Remember to place all group member names on each exercise)__

Exercise 2: Identify and Classify the System's Users

Analyze the system's users by creating a table to accomplish the following:
1. Classify each user as an end-user or as a user-manager.
2. Assess the commitment of each user to the systems development project.
3. Indicate how each user can be involved in the project: e.g., do some users have computer skills, business expertise, or other qualities that you can leverage as you develop the system?

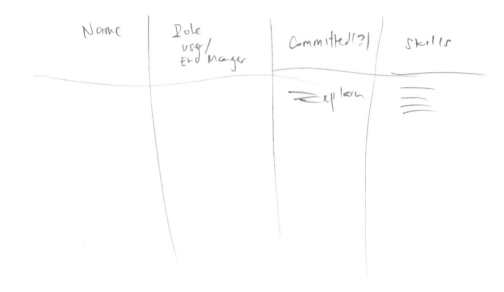

Exercise 3: Analysis of Interdependency of System Functions and System Components

Analyze the functions and components of the current system by creating and completing a Component Matrix that compares people to the other components in the system. Describe how the components work together using system functions. Within your explanation each interaction, use and underline the system functions.

YOUR FORMAT:

People	Procedures	Data	Software	Hardware
Person 1	In this box, describe how the person participates in procedures, and underline functions.	Et cetera . . .		
Person 2				
. . .				

Exercise 4: Workflow Diagrams & Affinity Diagram
(page 1 of 2)

1. Meet with your project team to assign each team member to draw a **user-level workflow diagram** based on an interview with one or more of the users. List each user-level workflow diagram and its creator in the space below:

User-Level WFD Title	Team Member Who Created WFD
Nastia Liukin - Prop warehouse clerk	Alexander Chung
Satya Swami - Set Designer	Christina Hoang
Shawn Mig - Lead Production Worker	thieu Nguyen

2. As a group, compile the user-level diagrams to **create a combined user-level workflow diagram** of the current system.
3. Clearly label your diagrams (providing a title for each, e.g., "User-level Workflow Diagram of Interview with _____") and attach them to this form.
4. On your combined user-level diagram, indicate the **system boundary**.
5. Based on your organization-level workflow diagram, **identify the major processes of the system**.

Exercise 4, Part 2: Workflow Diagrams & Affinity Diagram
(page 2 of 2)

1. **Analyze the combined user-level diagram** (a) to identify the internal and external entities of the current system and (b) to make a preliminary list of the system's workflows. **Relate each internal entity to the workflow(s) it creates (C) or uses (U) in the following matrix**.

Internal Entity ⇒ Workflow ⇓									

Exercise 5: Logical Process Model of the Existing System

1. Meet briefly with your team to confirm the major processes of the existing system, using your answer to Exercise 4, question 5 as your starting point.
2. *Working together*, specify the Level 0 Process Model of the existing system.
3. Then, assign one of these Level 0 processes to each team member. *Working individually*, create a balanced Level 1 (and lower levels, if necessary) Process Model to document the IPOSC functions of your assigned process in greater detail.
4. Process Models can be used to determine the input, processing, output, and storage functions of an information system. Analyze the child Process Model (s) you individually created to state the IPOSC requirements of your segment of the system.
5. Attach your Level 1 (and lower) Process Model s to this form. Submit all team member exercises together with your team's Level 0 Process Model.

Child DFD(s) of Process _____
(Process ID number and process description label)

Input Functions -- The system must accept the following inputs:

Processing Functions -- The system must perform the following processes:

Output Functions -- The system must generate the following outputs:

Storage Functions -- The system must maintain the following data:

Control Functions -- The system must enforce the following controls:

Name _____

Exercise 6: Critical Success Factor Analysis

Consider five sources of critical success factors -- industry, competitive, environmental, temporal, and managerial – and compile a list of CSFs for the company. For each CSF, explain the importance of Information Systems to achieving critical success factors.

1) CSF 1
   a. IS influence . . .
   b. IS influence . . .
2) CSF 2

Et cetera . . .

Exercise 7: Class Diagram of the Overall System

1) INDIVIDUAL ASSIGNMENT: Meet briefly with your project team members to assign one of the system's sample source documents or reports to each member. Create a class diagram of the object classes in your assigned document/report, taking into consideration any additional data requirements identified through analysis of the user interviews. In your model, indicate the identifier of each object class (if any), the class's attributes, and the cardinality of each object relationship.
2) GROUP ASSIGNMENT: Combine your individual class diagrams into a combined diagram for the entire system.

Exercise 8: Physical Database Design

1. Attach a copy of the Class Diagram you created for Exercise 10. Then define the required tables by creating the relations indicated by your Class Diagram. Underline the primary key of each relation; indicate foreign keys using a squiggle-underline. Use both an underline and a squiggle-underline to indicate a data element that is both a primary key and a foreign key.

2. Does it appear that you should segment or aggregate any of the object classes or attributes in your relations? If so, redefine the appropriate relations here, and explain your justification for segmenting or aggregating.

(Remember to place all group member names on each exercise)

Exercise 9: System Behavior Design--Use Cases and UML Use Case Diagram

1. As a team, identify the use cases of the new system (suggestion – base them on user classes). Assign one use cases to each member.
2. Working individually, write your assigned use case(s) in the space below.
3. Underline use-case phrases that require system behaviors.
4. Define methods to perform these behaviors and assign each to the appropriate object class (i.e., create an object relationship model segment that also specifies object methods).
5. Write structured text process descriptions for two of your object methods.
6. Create a UML Use Case Diagram that represents all of your use cases and actors.

Exercise 10: UML Activity Diagrams

1. As a team, examine your use cases and assign each member a use case.
2. Then, each member will create an Activity Diagram based on his/her assigned use case.

Exercise 11: UML Sequence Diagrams

1. As a team, examine your use cases and assign each member a use case.
2. Then, each member will create a Sequence Diagram based on his/her assigned use case.

Exercise 12: UML State Diagrams

1. As a team, examine your use cases and assign each member a use case.
2. Then, each member will create a State Diagram based on his/her assigned use case.

Exercise 13: Hardware & Software Specifications
(page 1 of 2)

1. **Hardware Specifications.** Identify the key hardware devices that will be required. For each device, provide a general indication of the number of units required, the performance levels expected (e.g., processor type, MHz, RAM, disk capacity, print speed and quality), and, where appropriate, any unique specifications that may be needed.

Hardware Devices	# Units	Performance Level	Unique Specifications
Processor/ Computer			
Secondary Storage			
Peripherals			
Telecommuni-cations			

Exercise 14: Hardware & Software Specifications
(page 2 of 2)

II. **Software Specifications.** Assume that the organization has decided to purchase an application package as the software component of the new system. Review your IPOSC requirements and other exercises or documentation to identify criteria to use in your evaluation of alternative software packages. In the space provided, briefly justify your weight for each criterion.

Criterion	Justification
1.	
2.	
3.	
4.	
5.	
6.	
7.	
8.	

Exercise 15: Deployment Diagram

1. Review your hardware specifications and the physical layout of locations mentioned in the case. Prepare a deployment diagram based on on this information.

Exercise 15: Requirements Analysis

1. We will discuss the submission of your requirements analysis in class.
    IBM Requisite Pro will be used.

Exercise 16: Project Risk Evaluation

1.   Evaluate the risk of the project. To receive full credit for this exercise, use the Comments section to explain your ratings.

Project Risk Evaluation		
Factors Affecting Project Risk	**Rating**	**Comments**
1. Characteristics of the organization a. Has stable, well defined objectives?		
b. Is guided by an information systems plan?		
c. Proposed system fits plan & addresses organizational objectives?		
2. Characteristics of the info. system a. Model available/ clear requirements?		
b. Automates routine, structured procedures?		
c. Affects only one business area? (no cross-functional or interorganizational links?)		
d. Can be completed in < 1 year?		
e. Uses stable, proven technology?		
3. Characteristics of the developers a. Are experienced in chosen development methodology?		
b. Are skilled at determining functional requirements?		
c. Are familiar with technology and information architecture?		
4. Characteristics of the users a. Have business area experience?		
b. Have development experience?		
c. Are committed to the project?		
Total Points		

2.   Briefly describe strategies to minimize each of the risks identified in your project.